YOUR KNOWLEDGE HAS VALUE

- We will publish your bachelor's and master's thesis, essays and papers

- Your own eBook and book - sold worldwide in all relevant shops

- Earn money with each sale

Upload your text at www.GRIN.com and publish for free

Richards Macdonald

The Advantages and Disadvantages of E-Recruitment

GRIN Verlag

Bibliografische Information der Deutschen Nationalbibliothek:

Die Deutsche Bibliothek verzeichnet diese Publikation in der Deutschen Nationalbibliografie; detaillierte bibliografische Daten sind im Internet über http://dnb.d-nb.de/ abrufbar.

Dieses Werk sowie alle darin enthaltenen einzelnen Beiträge und Abbildungen sind urheberrechtlich geschützt. Jede Verwertung, die nicht ausdrücklich vom Urheberrechtsschutz zugelassen ist, bedarf der vorherigen Zustimmung des Verlages. Das gilt insbesondere für Vervielfältigungen, Bearbeitungen, Übersetzungen, Mikroverfilmungen, Auswertungen durch Datenbanken und für die Einspeicherung und Verarbeitung in elektronische Systeme. Alle Rechte, auch die des auszugsweisen Nachdrucks, der fotomechanischen Wiedergabe (einschließlich Mikrokopie) sowie der Auswertung durch Datenbanken oder ähnliche Einrichtungen, vorbehalten.

Imprint:

Copyright © 2012 GRIN Verlag GmbH
Druck und Bindung: Books on Demand GmbH, Norderstedt Germany
ISBN: 978-3-656-43757-4

This book at GRIN:

http://www.grin.com/en/e-book/214076/the-advantages-and-disadvantages-of-e-recruitment

GRIN - Your knowledge has value

Der GRIN Verlag publiziert seit 1998 wissenschaftliche Arbeiten von Studenten, Hochschullehrern und anderen Akademikern als eBook und gedrucktes Buch. Die Verlagswebsite www.grin.com ist die ideale Plattform zur Veröffentlichung von Hausarbeiten, Abschlussarbeiten, wissenschaftlichen Aufsätzen, Dissertationen und Fachbüchern.

Visit us on the internet:

http://www.grin.com/

http://www.facebook.com/grincom

http://www.twitter.com/grin_com

THE ADVANTAGES AND DISADVANTAGES OF E-RECRUITMENT

Content

Abstract 2
The Advantages and Disadvantages of E-recruitment 2
E-Recruitment 3
Strengths of E-recruitment 4
Weaknesses of E-recruiting 5
Conclusions 8
Reference List 10

Abstract

The application of traditional recruitment techniques do not suffice anymore and are also not well-timed in order to bring in satisfactory pool of competent candidates. Through early-1990s, with the progression associated with online technologies, many have experienced the particular shift for the traditional recruitment techniques to e-recruitment. The web-based recruitment blends software programs as well as infrastructure, in addition to resume repositories which assist the particular clients in their recruitment operations. Internet lookups are actually very popular among the people looking for work.

Resumes delivered via the web as well as through e-mail could be scanned to get key phrases, determining essential information, abilities, proficiency, as well as working experience, hence lowering hands-on procession and probable mistakes. This elevates the effectiveness around choosing competent as well as a trustworthy workforce, lowers long term turnover, and recruits completing online documents presumptively use much less resources compared to that that post papers application packages. Companies can access job hunters spanning the planet and usually get far more applications. The process is cheaper for companies and also more expedited. Even though career boards have the ability to deal with extremely high quantities of both people looking for work as well as employers, they tend to not achieve high quality. The systems are not simple and also harmless enough to be made use of by comparatively unskilled end users; they lack a 'personal feel', raise confidentiality, security, authentication, and cheating issues. The systems additionally discriminate against some applicants due to badly developed hiring platforms. Integration of e-recruiting with convectional recruiting may also be challenging and globalization further complicates assessment for applicants across borders.

The Advantages and Disadvantages of E-recruitment

Within the human resource administration circumstance, recruitment is often a means of finding as well as obtaining the best candidates for an institution. Fundamentally, the procedure entails looking for as well as bringing in a good pool with competent candidates making use of numerous achievable recruitment strategies. The traditional recruitment techniques employed by businesses include getting in touch with close friends or even worker recommendations, using executive search, making use of newsprint classified advertisements, among others. Anytime there are actually adjustments within corporation's policy, this

procedure persists to happen regularly to incorporate, sustain, or even re-adjust their particular labor force in respect to the company as well as human resource planning (Tong, 2009).

Because world-wide competitiveness is constant and also market sectors getting a lot more proficiency-intensive, the actual recruitment for skilled individual employees gets to be crucial, and bringing in the best candidates on the correct time gets more challenging than ever before. The application of traditional recruitment techniques do not suffice anymore and are also not well-timed in order to bring in satisfactory pool of competent candidates. Numerous companies currently have ventured into implementing advanced recruitment methods or even merging different recruitment techniques to appeal to these people. For instance, through merging classifieds adverts together with executive search, or even recruitment firms, among others to get recruitment; but that simply enhances the elevated of recruitment expenses for each hire. Through early-1990s, with the progression associated with online technologies, many have experienced the particular shift for the traditional recruitment techniques to web based recruitment or e-recruitment (Tong, 2009). This essay seeks to explore the application of Human Resources Information System (HRIS) in e-recruitment.

E-Recruitment

E-recruiters can be found in two versions: corporate recruiters and also third-party recruiters. Third-party recruiters tend not to limit varieties of work opportunities published by the employers or even pick out particular job hunters resumes. They work as the facility intended for lots of different recruitments. A lot more specific around recruitment are usually small niche recruiters. The third-party recruiters or even e-recruitment service companies are specialized within the web-based recruitment and offer expert employing strategies to their consumers. These kinds of employment solutions blend software programs as well as infrastructure, in addition to resume repositories which assist the particular clients in their recruitment operations. Corporate recruiters incorporate recruitment capabilities within their internet sites which permit job hunters to apply employment straight with the company, without the need of dealing with any "third-party" (Tong and Sivanand, 2004).

Strengths of E-recruitment

Internet lookups are actually very popular among the people looking for work. When graduate business institution alumni were being required to point out which employment lookup techniques were being the most beneficial to them in obtaining appealing employment offers, online employment search placed second - at the rear of personal networking, yet well before headhunters, paper adverts, and also a number of other strategies. The reputation associated with web-based hiring is probably unsurprising, considering the advantages it provides to candidates as well as employing agencies (Thompson, Braddy and Wuenschc, 2008).

Shilpa and Gopal (2011) sum the examples of the benefits of Web-based Hiring tend to be: employs prime talent, reduces hiring expenses, telescoping hiring lead time, bigger applicant group, remarkable geographical access, selecting job-websites as well as controlling employment postings, preparing a 'killer' employment posting, multi-website curriculum vitae collection.

Resumes delivered via the web as well as through e-mail could be scanned to get key phrases, determining essential information, abilities, proficiency, as well as working experience, hence lowering hands-on procession and probable mistakes. Additionally, what appears to be relevant to the particular industry, background records searches may also be accessible on the internet, which in turn makes it possible for better precision and also effectiveness around choosing competent as well as a trustworthy workforce. The process is time conserving, because a great deal more unqualified or even unsuitable candidates may be avoided, by means of web based contact, within the preliminary stages in the recruitment procedure. The process also has enhanced capability to focus on a particular audience, in that way lowering long term turnover (Shani and Tesone, 2010). For Xerox, database-lookup capabilities, an important rating algorithm, selection requirements as well as a job-posting algorithm increase applicant sources and supply shortlists swiftly (Pollitt, 2004).

Internet resources may be taken advantage of in order to steer people looking for work towards ideal vacancies, and they also may convenience application logistics. The much less apparent advantage for Devonport Management Limited has been around the grade of applicants asked to evaluation centers. By using old techniques, the success rate of somewhere between 20 and 30 % of applicants would be the tradition. The actual success rate in 2007 was somewhere between 50 and 60 percent (Thompson, Braddy and Wuenschc,

2008; Leftley, 2007).

Recruits completing online documents presumptively incur much less expenses (in regard to time as well as funds) compared to that that post papers application packages. In the perspective of the employment hunter, through the use of technology they are able to currently seek out a wide selection of opportunities by distinct requirements, for instance place, placement type, placement specifications, as well as earnings (Thompson, Braddy and Wuenschc, 2008; Shani and Tesone, 2010). The program at SAT Telecom allows external candidates to submit an application for precise work opportunities as well as to generate a lot more general, speculative employment applications directly by means of the employment web page in the corporation's website. The particular front-end on the work portal is actually user friendly when it comes to get around (Pande, 2011).

Additionally, businesses can easily make use of the Web in order to evaluate résumés and also get in touch with potential job hopefuls. They are able to additionally include recruitment WebPages in prevailing organizational websites in order to entice applicants through marketing placement opportunities as well as advertising themselves to job hunters spanning the planet. Employers usually get far more applications, which usually brings about a larger group of applicants to choose from (Thompson, Braddy and Wuenschc, 2008; Shani and Tesone, 2010).

E-recruitment acts towards reducing spending, since it is actually considerably less expensive to advertise on the web as compared to inside a paper. When compared to the utilization of specialized search organizations the actual sums saved are actually greater. Recruiters may also obtain applications more rapidly; typically even about the same working day a placement is usually publicized (Shani and Tesone, 2010). According to Nike, who adopted e-recruitment in July of 2002, the typical period to fill up vacancies seems to have decreased from 62 days to 42 days. Financial savings of close to 54% in hiring expenses are actually acknowledged ever since the procedure was launched, and also there's been much less dependence on outside hiring as well as search firms due to the 'future interest' repository (Pollitt, 2005).

Weaknesses of E-recruiting

Even though career boards have the ability to deal with extremely high quantities of both people looking for work as well as employers, they tend not to, on their own, remedy the

issue associated with quality. Achieving a standardized range of top quality applicants on the internet is really a target yet still to become actualized for the majority of corporate and business end users (Bartram, 2000).

A significant movement within employees' management continues to be the particular decentralization associated with numerous functional obligations to personnel within enterprise unit, departmental or even line-management level. This particular development towards transference of obligation of hiring as well as assortment away to line administration has ramifications for any design associated with applicant assortment programs. It really is not anymore harmless to suppose that only a few trained office staff specialists will certainly oversee the actual hiring as well as assortment processes inside their company. Provided that these kinds of concrete realities exist, the task for work-related psychologists can be to model resources which are objective, as well as job-relevant, but additionally simple and also harmless to be made use of by comparatively unskilled end users (Bartram, 2000).

Seeing that e-recruitment will become much more of an information digesting plant, there exists a hazard that companies may well shed the 'personal feel' that might dissuade particular candidates. Investigation has discovered the fact that companies were being eager to keep up the personal feel in addition to taking advantage of technological innovation to bring in and also hire graduates. It should additionally always be appreciated that a few people looking for work might possibly not have easy access to the online world. Some, that happen to be much less acquainted with IT, might also be deterred when they experience technological complications unsupported. Using the Internet in order to appeal to fresh employees may consequently not really go well with most job hunters or even be suitable for filling up all of the vacancies and could cause constraining of the prospective applicant group (Barber, 2006).

Security issues come up with regards to safeguarding the particular examination publisher's and also writer's intellectual property privileges and in making sure that the security and safety of individuals private information is upheld. Additionally, confidentiality considerations come up with regards to making certain the examination taker's answers are kept in complete confidence and only revealed to individuals with the right and also a need to find out. Additional problems include: authentication to make sure that the individual taking the particular examination is definitely the individual they claim they really are; control of examination situations, to make certain there is absolutely no meltdown associated

with service while in the heart of the examination session as well as make sure that they're taking the particular examination unaided; control of practice, to guarantee that most examination takers have experienced adequate practice, without having these individuals getting over-exposed to precise examination content; equal rights to admittance, to make certain that appropriate populations of employment candidates get equal admission to the web (Bartram, 2000).

The Times Top 100 companies spent a lot of time as well as energy to make sure they would not discriminate against the increasing quantity of graduates getting into the actual broader and much more varied skills pool. Nevertheless, through implementing elementary proxies like degree type or even UCAS marks to lessen all the huge quantities of applications, they potentially risk not including numerous graduates that get into higher education by means of unique avenues. It has specific ramifications for graduates coming from non-conventional academic backdrops like specific ethnic minority communities (Barber, 2006).

The growing use, as well as, reputation associated with web-based hiring may also risk discriminating handicapped applicants in the event that companies don't know any ramifications belonging to the Disability Discrimination Act of 1995 with regard to web-based hiring. Organizations need to ensure individuals having handicaps can easily make application for employment through a different channel in the event that web-based techniques are certainly not accessible. Employers may well reduce female applicants due to badly developed hiring platforms: Graduate employers have experienced a decrease in female candidates ever since switching to a web-based system. The shortage of any personal feel additionally seemed to put women off (Barber, 2006).

Generally there may also be concerns whenever running web-based and also off-the-internet platforms together for exactly the same vacancies, since the pace belonging to the Web-based system might not be getting totally taken advantage of due to the added time necessary to get as well as process conventional paper-based applications. Additional legitimate complications for companies may be a consequence of deficiencies in Human Resources' understanding of working with e-recruitment as well as having a rigid software package. Aligning and combining web-based hiring together with additional Human Resources administration platforms, especially when it comes to compatibility together with versatility may also be challenging. This is especially valid in the event that companies tend to be dependent on the supplier's versatility to change their own offerings (Barber, 2006).

An additional group of concerns to take into account pertains to the globalization associated with assessment. There's currently an array of feasible geographical layouts with regard to examination-taker, examination, examination manager as well as the consumer Corporation. This kind of likelihood raises a number of queries, such as: which nation's examination benchmarks along with rules of practice are applicable; who the particular examination end user might be; the way the examination provider determines about end-user qualification concerns; within which nation the particular examination taker should have their particular qualification; and also the place that the obligation is placed with regard to making sure that the particular examination is tailored for the customs and also the dialect belonging to the examination taker, and that also the particular review generated is suitable for that client. Moreover, an issue crops up about the redress that examination taker possesses should they come to feel they've been handled unfairly, and also to exactly who, in which nation (Barber, 2006).

Conclusions

E-recruiters can be found in two versions: corporate recruiters and also third-party recruiters. The web-based recruitment blends software programs as well as infrastructure, in addition to resume repositories which assist the particular clients in their recruitment operations. Internet lookups are actually very popular among the people looking for work. Resumes delivered via the web as well as through e-mail could be scanned to get key phrases, determining essential information, abilities, proficiency, as well as working experience, hence lowering hands-on procession and probable mistakes. This elevates the effectiveness around choosing competent as well as a trustworthy workforce, lowers long term turnover, and recruits completing online documents presumptively use much less resources compared to that that post papers application packages. Companies can access job hunters spanning the planet and usually get far more applications. The process is cheaper for companies and also more expedited. Even though career boards have the ability to deal with extremely high quantities of both people looking for work as well as employers, they tend to not achieve high quality.

The systems are not simple and also harmless enough to be made use of by comparatively unskilled end users, they lack a 'personal feel' that might dissuade particular candidates, raise confidentiality, security, authentication and cheating issues. The systems

additionally discriminate against some applicants, such as ethnic minorities, the handicapped and female applicants due to badly developed hiring platforms. Integration of e-recruiting with convectional recruiting may also be challenging. Globalization further complicates assessment for applicants across borders.

Reference List

Bartram, D., 2000. Internet Recruitment and Selection: Kissing Frogs to find Princes. *International Journal Of Selection And Assessment, 8*(4), pp.261-274.

Barber, L., 2006. *E-Recruitment Developments.* Brighton: Institute for Employment Studies.

Leftley, A., 2007. E-recruitment delivers return on investment for DML. *Strategic HR Review, 6*(40), pp.8-9.

Pande, S., 2011. E-recruitment creates order out of chaos at SAT Telecom: System cuts costs and improves efficiency. *Human Resource Management International Digest, 19*(3), pp.21-23.

Pollitt, D., 2004. E-recruitment helps Xerox to pick the cream of the crop. *Human Resource Management International Digest, 12*(5), pp.33-35.

Pollitt, D., 2005. E-recruitment gets the Nike tick of approval. *Human Resource Management International Digest, 13*(2), pp.33-35.

Shani, A. and Tesone, D. V., 2010. Have human resource information systems evolved into internal e-commerce? *Worldwide Hospitality and Tourism Themes 2*(1), pp. 30-48.

Shilpa, V. and Gopal, R, 2011. The Implications Of Implementing Electronic- Human ResourceManagement (E-HRM) Systems In Companies. *Journal of Information Systems and Communication, 2* (1), pp-10-29.

Tong, D. Y., 2009. A study of e-recruitment technology adoption in Malaysia. Industrial Management & Data Systems, 109(2), pp.281–300.

Tong, D. Y and Sivanand, C, N., 2004. E-recruitment service providers review. Employee Relations, 27(1), pp. 103-117.

Thompson, L. F., Braddy, P. W. and Wuenschc, K. L., 2008. E-recruitment and the benefits of organizational web appeal. *Computers in Human Behavior, 24*(5), pp.2384-2398.